The Boneyard

Tiffany Grandstaff

BookLeaf Publishing

Presentation by *BookLeaf Publishing*

Web: www.bookleafpub.com

E-mail: info@bookleafpub.com

ISBN: 9789358368550

First edition 2023

To Dink & Toots for giving my life purpose and prose

ACKNOWLEDGEMENT

I would like to express my deepest gratitude to all the people who supported me during the creation of "The Boneyard." Your support and understanding helped me to find the courage to explore the darker aspects of life and to express my emotions through poetry.

Finally, I would like to acknowledge the poets and writers who have inspired me over the years and whose works have provided me with the motivation and inspiration to confront all sides of the universal human experience.

This collection is as much yours as it is mine.

PREFACE

This collection of poems emerged from a deep well of mixed emotions within the author's soul. These poems are a reflection of the universal human experience.

Throughout the process of writing this collection, the author explored the darker aspects of life, delving into the complex emotions that arise from witnessing the impermanence of all things.

"The Boneyard" is not an easy read, but it is a necessary one. The poems contained within these pages challenge the reader to confront their own mortality and the fleeting nature of existence. Amidst the darkness, the author hopes to shine a light on essential yet overlooked blessings.

"The Boneyard" is a tribute to the resilience of the human spirit and a testament to the power of poetry to provide meaning and understanding in the face of life's greatest challenges.

Dust & Stones

At dusk, a place of shadows
Where dead decay beneath and below,
Silent sentinels standing still,
Watching the sunset over the hill

Headstones like soldiers lined in a tight row
Testaments to lives lived once long ago
Each mound, a memoir of gain and loss,
Etched in stone, the ultimate cost

With the air still, the sky aglow,
Shadows lengthen, and night winds blow,
Whispers of trees, rustling grass,
A hint of something that will not pass

For here is quiet, hallowed ground,
Where the veil between is thin and round
Visit the boneyard if you dare,
To siphon mortality from the air

In this place of shadows and bones,
We are all but dust and stones.

You Drive Me CrAzY

You drive me crazy.
And when I'm feeling lazy,
You are the supplier,
That takes me higher than I've ever flown
before.
My feet no longer touch the floor; I soar.
Above the clouds and below my pride,
You are a magical mystery ride.

Dear You,

Dear You,

I cuss and I kick and I scream and I wail and I lose all my patience and I pull on my hair and I yell and I bitch and I moan and I spit and...I seriously wish that was it.

I'm not perfect and I'm not clean and I'm not able to say what I mean and I don't have time and I probably could and I won't say sorry, although I probably should.

We love and we fight and we laugh and we cry and we make love well into the night. But you see the real me, you feel me. We can't lie to save our lives.

Let's say goodbye and let's wave the white flag and let's chalk up to the best we ever had and let's complain and let's compare and let's poke our eyes out before we stare.

You can but I can't and you breathe while I pant and you will but I won't and I do but you don't.

Love,
Me

Hey God

Hey God, can you hear me up there?
I've prayed to you a thousand times from down
here.
You must not be able to hear me, Sarge.
The world is in chaos; who's in charge?
My requests have fallen on deaf ears,
It's not your will, or so I hear.
Present me with your guilded grace, my king
And wipe this misery off my face, I sing

Hey God, do you like poetry instead?
You won't answer when I pray in bed.
I don't know the doctrine, and I don't know the
code,
So by all means, overlook my abode.
You make no mistakes; just a happy accident,
I'm collateral damage in your earthly torment
And should I escape to rest without religion,
You'll send me to burn with your all-knowing
grin.

Look Away

When you're not looking, I keep a secret,
And perhaps I'll never let it show.
That when you're least expecting it, my love for
you grows...
    In the car
    While you sleep
    As you're busy thinking of everything but
me.
When you're not looking, I let out a sigh,
And perhaps I'll never tell you why.
But I doubt you could ever understand...
    Your gravity
    Our orbit
    Or the power of your hand.
When you're not looking, my lies become true,
Splayed on the stage, as if I could hide from
you.

Pirate's Booty

Ya know,
I can't help but smile,
After a little while,
Of you telling me I'm pretty,
Dressed in my nitties and gritties.
You still wax poetic about my beauty,
Staring at me and not my booty,
Although I appreciate that too...
I also see the beauty in you.

Ode to Jeramyah

My heart aches for you,
And those peculiar things you do,
And those chubby cheeks,
And how it's been weeks since I've seen them.

This world offers nothing to replace
That precious face,
That pitter-patter,
That joy that lingered long after we said our
goodbyes.

The pain that followed brought me to my knees,
Losing faith while begging please,
My victory
My surrender
My fate to remain the pretender.

(v): Prosper

To prosper:

to prevail,
to prevent,
to progress,
to lament,
to obtain,
to abstain,
to acquire,
to explain,
to believe,
to achieve,
to develop,
to perceive,
to access,
to profess,
to desire,
to possess.

Dawn's Crack

O, how does that sun muster the strength to
make each day begin,
As it rests on the horizon to torture me again.
Dawn's crack is showing with no disclosure,
Nature's indecent UV exposure.
O, how its existence discourages mine,
With a bright reminder of the march of time.
Another morning, afternoon, and night,
Early torment, late delight.

Cruise Blues

Along we stray from the city, highway lights
By the grasses, flowers - greens and whites
Dew on the petals, rot on the root
Life before death, then transmute

Through my perception, across my eyes
Whipping breezes, the clouds on high
Weeping willows, sullen blue sky
Drooping above me in a proud disguise

Cotton Curtain

Your beauty rests beyond your clothes,
Which therein lies the one I chose,
Laid bare behind a cotton curtain,
Perfect geometry, I am certain.

Your beauty hides beyond your style,
Resting instead inside your smile,
Which lingers for just a little while before
returning to its original domicile.

Your beauty stands beyond your figure,
Priceless like a Rembrandt picture,
Exquisitely ahead of your time,
And currently adored in mine.

Solitary ConFINEment

I bang my head against these walls
For reverberation to capture your attention,
With cries left silent as morning doves
Bouncing back as though never mentioned.

I call into the void like it will answer my
question
With ears perked for an echo of existence,
But what weight does my weightlessness
possess?
And why, then, all the resistance?

Forced presence, no presents, all grit, all gore.
Solitary con,
I'm fine,
Meant for nothing more.

Hate to Love

I hate beautiful things because I can't find the
time to love them.
They pass through a hurried gaze before my face
ever contorts,
My stone-cold stare pasted like a billboard of
emptiness,
Delaying expressions wrought from deep in my
core,
Hiding evidence of the person I am beneath
survival instincts.
Blurry shadows of beautiful things lie just
outside my reach,
Swaying lazily in the whipping winds that set
unbalance to my feet,
With borrowed air from beguiling breezes to
forfeit my abundance,
Accepting a fate as the residue of beautiful
things in decay.

Poetree

Wrinkled skin of the essence within,
Feverish ferver flowing through storied veins.

Branches burning with thirsty roots yearning,
Patient for dark clouds to yield rain.

The boastful splendor of a legal tender,
Reduced to foating ashes of its remains.

Don't Mind Me

15

Why change clothes when I can't change your
mind?
Why pour a cup of coffee or open the blinds?
Who's looking at me when you're not around?
Where am I headed if you can't be found?

I won't utter a word because you won't listen.
I won't shed a tear for light to steal and glisten.
You'll never look in the rearview mirror.
And I'll always be left standing here...

Don't mind me as I spiral out of control
And lose my identity destroying what I know
To become a fleeting figment of my own
imagination,
Setting things on fire to avoid the stagnation.

Daddy Long Legs

You're not serious,
This can't be real.
I know I told you how it makes me feel.

Your lies consume us,
They turn passion to pain.
I'm not sure what's real or feigned.

Your silk spins sharply, Daddy Long Legs,
There's no relationship left to destroy.
You can't treat the web of love like it's a toy.

Cling high on the door jamb,
Observe my scurries from afar.
That's where you settled, stay where you are.

Your venom doesn't scare me,
It's hardly poison at all.
I'll slam the door just to watch you fall.

I'm trapped in your web, Daddy Long Legs,
But I won't be here for long.
This isn't what I meant when I said prove me
wrong.

Riot in My Head

It's too quiet
Now I riot
In my head
Thinking of going back to bed.
I need miracles to start showing
And a little something to get me going
Out of the covers in this dark abode
Back on my feet to hit the road.
Give me a pill to knock back
Put blinders on the things I lack
Give me a match to set this place on fire
Because you're a saint and I'm a liar.
We collide like water and oil
Our passions rage
To a bittersweet boil
I swear
It's like neither one of us cares.
So do you mind if just for today
I stay
Lay
Pray
Grow old
Turn grey
In this cold and empty bed?
There's a riot in my head.

Legend of the Fall

She said, "Love wasn't put in our hearts to stay,
because love isn't love until we give it away."
So she gave and gave and gave and gave
Emptying her vessel to become love's slave

Legends say you can hear a heartbeat's echo
with an ear upon her chest
So they test and test and test and test
Perceiving only what's blatantly manifest

No Receipt

You told me not to worry about what you were
doing
While we were screwing,
But your hate was brewing.
You said not to fret about the things you said
While they rattled in my head,
Birthing resentment stirring dread.
You asked me to rebuild the bridges you burned
While my heart quietly yearned,
Then the tables got turned.
You promised not to throw me under the bus
While we split up to discuss,
Us.
You lied about everything you are and are not
I was trapped in ruminating thought,
But you finally got caught.
You sleep on a bed made of concrete
While I toss and turn trying to copy and delete,
This goodbye is so bittersweet.
You stole my time and changed my mind
While our hearts were still intertwined,
And now your credit gets declined.

Ghosthunter

Ghosts are real, although some not deceased.
They wander around the grocery store, adding
up receipts.
They stroll along the walkways talking to
themselves.
Uninspired to live, unwilling to delve.
They fill up libraries, movie theaters, and halls.
They scoot to the side and slink along walls.
Their hurried dismissal as a badge of dishonor,
The life of a ghost without being a goner.

www.ingramcontent.com/pod-product-compliance
Lightning Source LLC
LaVergne TN
LVHW050506210726

843509LV00015BA/3008